ATTITUDE
OF A
Servant

Today 09/10/2014

ATTITUDE
OF A
Servant

Dr. Michael Landsman

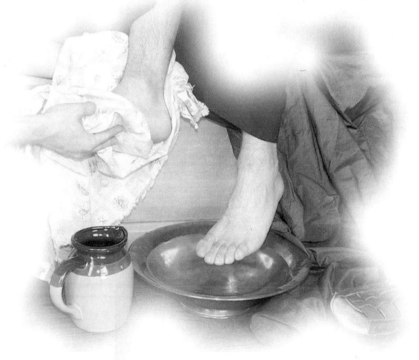

Bridge-Logos *Publishers*

Gainesville, Florida 32614 USA

ATTITUDE OF A SERVANT
by Dr. Michael Landsman

Bridge-Logos *Publishers*
P.O. Box 141630
Gainesville, FL 32614
www.bridgelogos.com

94 93 92 91 90 89 88 87   0 9 8 7 6 5 4 3 2 1

International Standard Book Number: 0-88270-9038

Unless otherwise indicated, all scripture quotations have been
taken from the King James version of the Bible.

Scripture quotations marked AMP are taken from *The Amplified
Bible, New Testament* ©1954, 1958, 1987 by The Lockman
Foundation. Used by permission.

This book is printed on acid-free paper.

Table of Contents

Dedication

This book is dedicated to my lovely wife and help-meet, Martha. I could never have written it without her encouragement and support. Her steadfast belief and confidence in me is a constant source of strength. She, above all others, is a great example of living the lifestyle of or having the attitude of a servant.

Preface

While preparing to write this book, my mind went back to the various individuals who have had dramatic effects upon my life. All of them had one thing in common: the attitude of a servant. The whole desire of these people was to obey God's call upon their lives and to help people.

My first pastor was a great influence upon me. He taught me discipline and commitment to God and to His Church.

There are several other men and women of God who have had a great impact on my life. They instilled in me the integrity of God's work as being His will for us. They inspired and counseled, but most all were friends who encouraged me in my spiritual walk and growth in God.

The one thing these people demonstrated was the attitude to serve. To serve God and to serve God's people, for there is no real service to God apart from serving His people.

In Ephesians 4:11-16, we see a marvelous depiction of the purpose of what has been called the five-fold ministry: the apostle, the prophet, the evangelist, the pastor, and the teacher. They are given as gifts to the Church, and gifts are given to be used. In this case, to serve the Church so it will mature and grow into the fullness of what God called it to be.

It is to this end that I have written this book. It is part of my service to the Body of Christ, that we might grow and mature in our attitude and our service in the work of the Kingdom.

Introduction

There are some things in my heart that I desire to share with you, that can greatly impact and revolutionize your life and productivity for the Kingdom of God.

In the Gospels, Jesus provides vivid examples of how we should live. In His teachings, He stressed the attitudes of the heart, for God looks on the intent of the heart more than the outcome of the actions.

Jesus shows us a true servant, one who was determined to do the will of God from the heart. He demonstrates that having a servant's heart is not a sign of weakness, but rather a sign of strength and inner peace.

I am the type of individual who lives a challenge, even when it requires change on my part. I have found that God expects us to grow, and that means change. While change is mandatory, we must keep in mind that the principles of God remain constant, but the method of enacting those principles are variable and change with the dynamics in society.

Sociology tells us that our society is reinventing itself every 3-5 years. Have we in the Church kept pace with these changes? New methods do not necessarily change principles, but rather give us an opportunity to impact, win, and train people in a relevant way.

Television is a classic example of this principle. Sixty years ago, the idea of spreading the Gospel by television was absurd, but today television is a very practical and efficient tool for evangelism. The change was not in God or in His principles, but rather in our modern technology. Television, which at one time was considered a 'tool of the devil,' is now reaching millions of people with the Gospel. It has enabled us to be more effective in carrying out the Great Commission: to preach the Gospel to the entire world.

It is challenging to look at your lifestyle and service for the King and determine if your attitude and actions are equal to each other. For your actions must always be in correspondence to the proper attitude.

You can never be a true servant until you know your rights and privileges as well as your responsibilities. In Christian terms, a good servant completely identifies with the Master. To properly represent his master, a servant must be familiar with all that his master is. The servant's attitude directly affects his ability to serve his master in any situation.

Likewise, your attitude is one of the most vital aspects of your Christian life. Your attitude must be right in everything you do so that the Master's perfect will can be carried out.

It is my intent through this book, to help you to grow into all God has for you to be and do. That means continual upward movement, along with the proper attitude. I am confident that as you read this book, you will be enlightened by the Holy Spirit on how to be more productive in the Kingdom of God, while maintaining the *Attitude of a Servant*.

I AM Enlightened by the Holy Spirit.

1

The Right Attitude

The attitude you maintain determines the altitude at which you fly. Your attitude determines how high you're going to go, what you're going to do for God, and how successful you'll be in the Kingdom of God.

Proverbs 23:7 says, "For as he thinketh in his heart, so is he." We've used that verse in referring to faith confessions: "I've got to get the right attitude in my heart. I've got to see myself the way Jesus sees me. The only way I can do that is to view myself through the Word of God." That's true, but there's more to the right attitude than we previously thought.

Attitude is the most important thing you'll ever have to deal with. It will make you or break you. It will determine success or failure.

The word *attitude* is interesting. Webster's New Collegiate Dictionary defines attitude as "a mental position with regard to a fact or state." In other words, your attitude, or mental position, is produced by certain facts that you have. When you get new facts, therefore, your mental position should change. The 'facts' for a Christian are found in the Word of God. When you read the facts in God's Word, your attitude, your mental position, should change.

In Romans 12:1-2, Paul writes:

I beseech you therefore, brethren, by the
mercies of God, that ye present your bodies a
living sacrifice, holy, acceptable unto God,
which is your reasonable service.

And be not conformed to this world: but be
ye transformed by the renewing of your
mind, that ye may prove what is that good,
and acceptable, and perfect, will of God.

That first verse is interesting. He said, "I *beseech*
you." If you do a word study on *beseech*, you'll find that
it doesn't mean 'to beg.' It means "to present your case
in such a way that it produces the desired results in
individuals."

When you beg someone to do something, they
might or might not do it. But the Greek word for
beseech means that you present the request in such a
way that the other person has no alternative but to do
what you've asked. Paul didn't say, "I beg of you to do
this. I wish that you would do this." What he did was
present his case in such a way that they didn't have a
choice.

When I first began a traveling ministry, my family
traveled with me. We would go to a hotel at night, and
my wife would say, "Honey, you don't want to help me
get the kids ready for bed, do you?" And she got the
answer her question anticipated: "No."

Then she got hold of the meaning of the word
beseech, and instead of saying, "You don't want to, do
you?" she would say, "Honey, I need some help. Please
get the children ready for bed."

She was nice and sweet about it, but didn't leave
me the choice of saying, "No, I don't want to." My want

to was not involved at all. Now it was, "I need help. Please do it."

When Paul says, "I beseech you therefore, brethren, by the mercies of God," he is in essence saying: "I'm presenting this to you in such a way that you have no alternative but to do it. And the reason you have no alternative is because of all the mercies of God that you've received—salvation, healing, deliverance, baptism of the Holy Spirit, the gifts of the Spirit."

"He's given you His life, His nature, and His ability. He's caused you to be prosperous. All things are yours. In view of everything that God has done for you, in view of all the mercies of God, don't you think the least you could do is present your body as a living sacrifice?"

That puts the Scripture in a whole different light. The Amplified Bible helps to show this by stating that presenting your body as a living sacrifice to God "is your reasonable (rational, intelligent) service and spiritual worship."

My attitude should be, "God, I'm Yours. What do You want me to do? In view of all that You've done for me, what do You want me to do for You?" Paul's words in the next verse makes this clearer: "And be not conformed to this world: but be ye transformed by the renewing of your mind."

The word *transform* means to go through a complete metamorphosis, a complete change in kind, like the caterpillar that goes into a cocoon and comes out a butterfly. Basically, Paul is saying, "Don't be conformed to this world. Don't be conformed to the world's standard. Don't be conformed to the external or temporal pressures that come upon you. Be transformed, allow a complete metamorphosis to occur in your life by the renewal of your mind."

The Amplified Bible says it this way: "by the [entire] renewal of your mind by its new ideals and its new attitude." With a renewed mind, a new attitude, you're going to have a new ideal that sets a standard, a goal, a vision, in front of you of what you need to be.

NEW ATTITUDE AND NEW IDEALS

Your new attitude and new ideals will be determined by God, because your mind has been renewed by the Word of God.

The word *attitude* also means a position in relationship to a fixed point of reference. That's something I understand because I'm a pilot and love to fly. Flying can teach you some very important lessons.

In the airplane, there is an instrument with an artificial horizon. It shows a little airplane, the sky, and the ground. If you become enveloped in a cloud bank or lose visibility some other way, you'd better believe what that instrument shows you. Otherwise, you may think you're going in one direction when you're really going in another. You may think you're in a climbing turn to the left when you're actually descending to the right.

That instrument tells you whether you're going up or down, whether you're remaining on course, whether you're banked to the left or to the right. Even when all your senses tell you something else, you had better believe the instrument—it shows your position in relationship to your only fixed point of reference: the ground.

The Word of God is our instrument that shows us a fixed point of reference and our relationship to it. Your attitude is your position in relation to that fixed point of reference. Your attitude will determine your actions.

When I first began to study the attitude of a servant, God showed me that the emphasis was on

18

service, holiness, effectiveness, and purity of motive.
He showed me times in my life when I had opportunities
to exhibit this attitude.

I worked with the Los Angeles Police Department
as a chaplain for five and a half years. I didn't work in
the prisons. I worked on the front lines in patrol cars,
with barricaded suspects, with hostages, with attempted
suicides, or in family disputes—all the easy things!

After I'd been on the job a year, I saw a need in
the department for a set of uniform principles and
guidelines that could be followed by all our chaplains. I
wrote down my suggestions and presented them to one
of the commanders. He was nice and took me to lunch.
In other words, he humored me. But he said my suggestions were not needed.

About two years later, we had a day-long meeting
of all the chaplains. After everyone hashed out their
thoughts, they came up with recommendations. Their
suggestions were exactly what I'd presented two years
before to the commander.

This time, he changed things just a little bit from
what I'd given him and, "on the basis of their recommendations," presented a comprehensive program. It
became his project. I praised God because at least part
of what I saw as a great need was done. When you begin
to deal with effectiveness and motives, and your attitude
is one of service, it doesn't matter who gets the credit.

Later, I worked on developing a curriculum for a
Bible institute. When it was completed, it was taken and
used overseas. The introductory page highlighted the
curriculum, the school, and included a picture of the
staff. There was, however, no picture or mention of me,
even though I had created and written the entire curriculum.

My attitude was, "God, I get credit with You. And the main thing is that it's being used and that people's lives are going to be changed. That's what's important."

CONCEIT OR SELF-ESTEEM?

Now it's good to have a strong sense of identity. In fact, if you don't have a healthy self-esteem, you probably won't be very productive in the Kingdom of God. You need to have a strong spirit that says, "You can do it, you can do it, you can do it."

But you need to keep your ego—all the self things—in line with the Word. Saying, "I can do it because I can do all things through Christ who strengthens me," keeps you in the proper perspective compared to the Lord. (See Philippians 4:13.) "I can do it because of Christ. I can do it—and, praise God, look at what I've done."

Some may say, "Brother, I wouldn't talk like that." But in Matthew 25, the Parable of the Talents tells us that when the master reckoned with the servant, his answer was, "Lord, this is what I've done with what You've given me."

He didn't say, "I didn't do anything." He said, "You gave this to me, and I took it and produced twice as much." He recognized that it came from his Master, that it had been entrusted to Him, and that He had something to do with producing the result. You must have confidence in yourself.

After the Lord showed me this, I went to my pastor and said, "Pastor, I've just discovered I have a really big ego. But I've learned to determine what is me and what is God, and I know how to keep my ego in check."

He said, "That's good, because if you didn't have a large ego, you wouldn't be of any benefit or value to me." That's the difference between people who are self-motivated and people who must have supervisors constantly telling them what to do. People who are self-motivated have a strong sense of identity. They know who they are.

Romans 12:3 says, "For I say, through the grace given unto me, to every man that is among you, not to think of himself more highly than he ought to think."

That's why it's so important to understand the attitude of a servant. Once you develop this attitude, ego is no longer a problem. The attitude of a servant keeps pride and self-will from arising and keeps self in its proper place.

In my given Mission I have to Trust the owner of the work Jesus Christ for His and my Holy Father.
I AM confident in my ability skills — GoD Through Jesus. Christ has something to do with producing results —

2

Recreated to Work

Ephesians 6:5-8 says:

Servants, be obedient to them that are your
masters according to the flesh, with fear and
trembling, in singleness of your heart, as
unto Christ;

Not with eyeservice, as menpleasers; but as
the servants of Christ, doing the will of God
from the heart;

With good will doing service, as to the Lord,
and not to men:

Knowing that whatsoever good thing any
man doeth, the same shall he receive of the
Lord, whether he be bond or free.

The Amplified Bible translates "in singleness of
your heart" as "in singleness of motive." You should
write that in the margin of your Bible. The next verse in
the Amplified Bible says, "Not in the way of

ATTITUDE OF A SERVANT

eyeservice—as if they were watching you—and only to please men; but as servants (slaves) of Christ, doing the will of God heartily and with your whole soul." This is because "in singleness of motive" and "doing the will of God with your whole soul" both depict attitudes.

It's God's will that we serve. It's God's will that we work. Adam was created in the image and likeness of God. When Adam fell, a void was formed on the inside of man that can only be filled when he comes back into relationship with God. When you come back into this relationship, you're recreated.

Ephesians 2:10 says we are "created in Christ Jesus unto good works, which God hath before ordained that we should walk in them." You're recreated to work.

So you go out and begin to witness to people and share Christ with them. You tell them, "There's a God-shaped void on the inside of you, and it can only be filled when you're born again." They get born again, filled with the Spirit, and are just aglow.

Then, about two years later, if they haven't become involved in working within the Body, they're just as miserable as they were before becoming recreated. Why? When you talk to them, they say, "There's something missing. I don't know what it is. I thought when I received Jesus it would take care of that void in my life. What's wrong?"

Receiving Jesus did fill that God-shaped void. But, once that empty space was filled, and they didn't go on to become servants, they developed another void. God called us to serve. We are recreated "in Christ Jesus unto good works." If you don't work, there'll be a void, and you'll be miserable.

In Ephesians 6:6, Paul says, "doing the will of God from your heart." You're to work with singleness of motive, doing the will of God. "Well," you say. "What is the will of God?" WORK! "Why?" Because you're recreated "in Christ Jesus unto good works." You're recreated in Christ to work.

When I saw that, it put some things into perspective for me. I'm recreated to work. "Knowing that whatsoever good thing any man doeth, the same shall he receive from the Lord, whether he be bond or free" (Ephesians 6:8). Pauls saying to do the will of God with singleness of heart because you'll be rewarded by God.

REWARDS FROM GOD

Your reward doesn't come from man, but from God. So when you're working and serving with singleness of motive, whether you get any recognition from man doesn't matter. Whatever you do, you'll receive the same of the Lord.

My two oldest children, Michael and Linda, experienced a personal example of this some time ago. They accompanied my wife and me on a ministry trip to Holland and Norway.

While in Holland, we ministered for the Rev. Johan Maasbach at his World Mission in Der Haag. During our week with him, the children decided to help out with the work in the mission's tape room. They put labels on tapes and filled tape holders and cataloged tapes.

They were so excited about serving the Lord that they did not view it as work. In fact, we had to make them sit down and eat their meals. They wanted to just grab a quick bite and get back to work.

They were doing this on a voluntary basis, asking no pay nor expecting any. They were doing it out of a love for the Lord.

One night I told them, "The Lord will reward you for your labor of love for His name." I reminded them of Luke 6:38, "Give, and it shall be given unto you."

They were not working for a reward, but God rewards the faithful. (Ephesians 6:8, Proverbs 28:20.)

On our last day in Holland, my wife, Martha, went to the market place where you can buy anything from food to clothes to toys. While she was there, a woman approached her and said, "I have been in Bible school this week and have been so blessed by your ministry. I just bought these gifts for your children." With that, she handed Martha a large bag.

Martha brought the gifts back, and that evening we gave the lady's presents to the children. Michael's first comment was, "See, Linda, Daddy told us God would bless us for serving Him." He realized that the gifts really were from God for their service to Him.

They not only received satisfaction from a job well done, but received a reward in this world as well. Service with the right motive produces for the Kingdom of God and you.

THE MIND OF CHRIST

There's a familiar passage of Scripture in Philippians 2:5 that we haven't understood clearly in the past: "Let this mind be in you, which was also in Christ Jesus."

That means, you should let the mind—the thoughts, the attitudes, and the ideals—accept the standard that was in Christ Jesus be in you. Glory to God!

The sixth verse continues: "Who, being in the form of God, thought it not robbery to be equal with God."

We've heard this preached, and have become excited about it. We've said, "Praise God, the mind of Christ is in me. I do hold the thoughts and the intents and the purposes of God's heart. I've got the mind of Christ."

We've also said, "I've got the mind of Christ. I don't think it's robbery to be equal with God, because I'm a joint heir with Jesus." We've used that, among other verses, to prove that we've been made "the righteousness of God" (2 Corinthians 5:21).

And we were right, as far as we went. Psalm 82:6 says, "I have said, Ye are gods; and all of you are children of the most High." But that's god with a lower case "g." We were created in the image of God to rule and reign in this earth. And then we were recreated in Christ Jesus. He "thought it not robbery to be equal with God." We're equal with God in the sense that we're joint heirs with Jesus Christ. Because of our position in Him, we're equal with Jesus in that aspect.

But we skipped verses 7 and 8 of Philippians chapter 2 and went on to verses 9 and 10, which say: "Wherefore God also hath highly exalted him, and given him a name which is above every name: That at the name of Jesus every knee should bow."

We said, "God has highly exalted me and given me a name that is above every name. I have the name of Jesus. Everything must bow to the name of Jesus."

The verses we ignored, however, give the proper context for all this: "But made himself of no reputation, and took upon him the form of a servant, and was made in the likeness of men: And being found in fashion as a man, he humbled himself, and became obedient unto death, even the death of the cross."

Paul is saying that because of our position in Christ, we should make ourselves of no reputation. He is not saying we should exalt ourselves. The highly exalted part didn't come until after the humbling and obedience.

In Matthew 20:28, Jesus says, "Even as the Son of man came not to be ministered unto, but to minister." If He had wanted to be ministered to, He would have remained in heaven. But He came to minister, and so He made Himself "of no reputation."

You cannot make yourself "of no reputation" until you have a reputation. You can't make yourself "nothing" until you've been "something." Jesus was not concerned about anything. He was satisfied. He knew who He was, what He was to do, and, therefore, didn't need to make a reputation for Himself.

People who need to make a reputation for themselves and make their name known are insecure. Jesus was secure. When you're secure, you can make yourself of no reputation. If you're insecure, you have to have a reputation.

Jesus humbled Himself by being obedient. The best way for us to be humble is to learn to be obedient.

I come from a family of five children. We all had various chores to do around the house. When I was 16, I decided that housework was 'women's work'. I told this to my dad.

I thought that now I was a man and didn't need to scrub floors or wash windows or do any other type of 'women's work'. I was in for a rude awakening. My dad let me know in no uncertain terms that helping around the house was not 'women's work'.

He told me all of the chores were done by the family working together to achieve a common goal. He made a statement that had a lasting impact on my spirit. He said, "If doing so-called 'women's work' makes you feel less of a man, then you're in trouble. You're insecure inside yourself and in your masculinity."

That statement is so true. If you're secure within yourself, what you do or how you function doesn't determine who you are. We are to be totally identified with Christ. Because of that, it doesn't matter what job we do for Him.

Once, when an evangelist ministered to the staff of our church, he said to me, "Be humble, be humble, be humble." So I started examining my life. I talked with him afterward, and he said, "The Lord wasn't displeased. He was just giving you advice for the future."

He brought up the subject again a few months later and said, "The Lord wasn't displeased with you, or telling you that you weren't humble. He was just reminding you to stay that way." So I told God, "You know I want to stay humble and obedient. I don't want false humility, nor do I want to walk below my rights and privileges. I want to walk fully in what You have for me."

As long as we have the mind of Christ in this way—by being humble and obedient—we can serve Him in the way He wants, and be and do all He has for us. In this mindset, we are poised to use all our talents and abilities to their fullest.

3

The Parable of the Talents

While I was studying the Word of God one day, a portion of Scripture seemed to stand out. In it I found God's plan for doubling our ability and productivity in the kingdom of God. That portion of Scripture is Matthew 25:14-30. It reads:

For the kingdom of heaven is as a man traveling into a far country, who called his own servants, and delivered unto them his goods.

And unto one he gave five talents, to another two, and to another one; to every man according to his several ability; and straightway took his journey.

Then he that had received the five talents went and traded with the same, and made them other five talents.

And likewise he that had received two, he also gained other two.

But he that had received one went and
digged in the earth, and hid his lord's money.

After a long time the lord of those servants
cometh, and reckoneth with them.

And so he that had received five talents came
and brought other five talents, saying, Lord,
thou deliveredst unto me five talents: behold,
I have gained beside them five talents more.

His lord said unto him,

Well done, thy good and faithful servant:
thou hast been faithful over a few things, I
will make thee ruler over many things: enter
thou into the joy of thy lord.

He also that had received two talents came and
said, Lord, thou deliveredst unto me two talents: behold,
I have gained two other talents beside them.

His lord said unto him,

Well done, good and faithful servant; thou
hast been faithful over few things, I will
make thee ruler over many things: enter thou
into the joy of thy lord.

Then he which had received the one talent
came and said, Lord, I knew thee that thou
art an hard man, reaping where thou bast not
sown, and gathering where thou hast not
strawed:

and I was afraid, and went and hid thy talent
in the earth: lo, there thou hast that is thine.

His lord answered and said unto him,

Thou wicked and slothful servant, thou
knewest that I reap where I sowed not, and
gather where I have not strawed:

Thou oughtest therefore to have put my
money to the exchangers, and then at my
coming I should have received mine own
with usury.

Take therefore the talent from him, and give
it unto him which hath ten talents.

For unto every one that path shall be given,
and he shall have abundance: but from him
that hath not shall be taken away even that
which he hath.

And cast ye the unprofitable servant into
outer darkness: there shall be weeping and
gnashing of teeth.

Many who read this parable have a preconceived
idea concerning the talents. They think the talents still
belonged to the master after he had given them to his
servants. This is not so, and such thinking will prejudice
our understanding of this parable. It is important that we
let the Word speak for itself.

In this parable, Jesus is teaching His disciples (and
us) how to double their ability in the kingdom of
heaven.

The term *kingdom of heaven* or *kingdom of God*
has a very definite meaning in the Scriptures. It refers to
our living in the totality of the rule of the Lord upon this
earth. When Jesus taught about the kingdom, He was
teaching how to operate in the principles that govern the

operation of the sphere of God's dominion and rule. (See Matthew 16:19; 18:18; Ephesians 2:6).

The word kingdom carries two distinct meanings when used in the New Testament. First, "the sphere of dominion." Second, "the activity of reigning."[1] This second meaning, "the activity of reigning," carries three basic elements: (1) bringing deliverance, (2) conferring blessings, and (3) exercising authority.

When we understand that the kingdom of heaven is the activity of reigning, then we can better understand the parables of Jesus. When He is teaching that the kingdom of heaven is like unto, He is telling us that this parable will teach us how to operate in the activity of reigning. In the above passage from Matthew's Gospel, we can see that Jesus is instructing His disciples on how to operate in the activity of reigning.

By taking this portion of Scripture and examining it piece by piece, we can see how to operate in the kingdom of heaven.

In verse 14 we read, "and delivered unto them his goods." Notice the word delivered. It means "to deliver over, to surrender, to yield up." It is the same word used in Romans 8:32 when speaking of God delivering up His Son for us. When something (or someone) is delivered, it becomes the property of the one to whom it is delivered.

Jesus was delivered up for us. He is ours and we are His. This can also be seen in Ephesians 5:25, where the word gave is the same word as translated delivered in Matthew 25.

In our text, verse 15 tells us that the goods were portioned out to the servants. One man received five, one received two, and one received one. According to this verse in The Amplified Bible, each man was given "in proportion to his own personal ability."

TALENT

A *talent* is a monetary measurement, which today is approximately the equivalent of $1,000. That would be a fortune in Jesus' day.

The average wage was a *penny* per day, a penny being worth 15 cents. The average worker earned $54.75 a year, which was considered a livable wage.

In this relation, you can see that the master delivered a small fortune to each of his servants. The first man was given $5,000, the second man, $2,000, and the third man, $1,000. Each man was given in proportion to his own personal ability to use it—no more and no less.

It is important to understand that each man had the ability to use what was delivered to him. They were not asked to go beyond their ability, but to operate within the scope of the ability they had.

Have you ever been asked to become involved with some aspect of your church? You might have been asked to serve as host or hostess, counselor, usher, or maybe even teacher of the toddlers' class. You were not being asked to do a job held by someone else, but rather to do something for the kingdom of God according to the ability you have.

In the parable we have read, each individual was given according to his several ability, his own personal ability. God will never ask you to do beyond the ability you possess in Him, nor will He ask you to do less than the ability you have.

In another rendering of this parable, Luke 19:12-26, we can find further clarification of this principle. Luke 19:13 reads, "delivered unto them ten pounds, and said unto them, 'Occupy till I come.'" The word occupy means "to enter into transaction; to do business; to trade; to enter into commerce." In other words, each man was given the talents (money) to enter into commerce according to his ability.

When each man received the talents, they became his. They were no longer the master's; they became the servant's. We have looked at this parable religiously and thought the master demanded the talents and the increase from each man when he reckoned with them. This is not so. They were no longer the master's once he gave them to the servants.

In Matthew 25:16-18 we see what each individual did with the money he had received. The man who had received the five talents ($5,000) traded with the same. He entered into commerce and made an additional $5,000. The man who had received the two talents ($2,000) did the same, and he gained another $2,000. The man who received the one talents ($1,000) hid his lord's money in the earth.

Then the master of the servants returned and reckoned with them (verse 19). This is where we tend to become bogged down with traditional thinking. Most think that when the Lord reckoned with His servants, He wanted both His money and the money they had gained. That is not so. According to Webster's 20th Century Unabridged Dictionary, the word reckon means "to explain, to tell, to make a reckoning." The word reckoning means "a settlement of rewards; a measuring of possibilities for the future.

That brings the meaning of this point of the parable into a clearer focus. The master had quite a lot held in reserve for these servants, but they were given an initial amount, to see how they would perform. The blessings of the future are built upon the faithful and consistent use of what you have now.

Your future will be determined by how you use what is currently in your hand. The life you have now is a direct result of the choices you have made and the use of what has been entrusted into your hands.

Here in Matthew 25, the master of these servants was asking for an accounting of what the men had done with a view to future plans and possibilities. He was not asking for the money (talents). He just wanted to know what the men had done with the money so he could reward them for their faithfulness.

I want you to notice the attitude among these servants. Each man was given according to his own personal ability. The first two men had the same attitude when they reckoned with the master. Both said, "You delivered unto me, and I have gained." Both had received the money as their own and were relating what they had done with it, what they had accomplished.

A SERVANT ATTITUDE

The attitude of some believers today is one of false humility. They say, "Brother, I would never say 'I have done something.' It was God, and I wouldn't want to share His glory." This sounds good and seems right, but it is a subtle form of deception. It is true that without God we could do nothing, but we are not without Him. We "can do all things through Christ who strengthens us" (Philippians 4:13).

We are accountable for what we do with the abilities God has given us. We are to boldly say, "You have given to me, and I have done this with it." This attitude is pleasing to God. Remember, the parable in Matthew 25 is teaching us how to operate in the kingdom of God.

The Lord did not rebuke these men and say they were egotistical and boastful. He did not punish them for having a prideful attitude. He said, in essence, "Well done, you good and faithful servant. You are to be commended for using what I gave you to the best of your ability. You have been faithful over a few things; I will make you ruler over many things. Enter into the joy of your Lord."

Now let us look at the attitude of the third servant. This man dug a hole in the earth and hid his lord's money. (Matthew 25:18.) But it was not his lord's money, it was his. The money had been delivered to him. He displayed a very poor attitude that became even more pronounced when the master asked for an accounting.

> Then he which had received the one talent
> came and said, Lord, I knew thee that thou
> art a hard man, reaping where thou hast not
> sown, and gathering where thou hast not
> strawed:
>
> and I was afraid, and went and hid thy talent
> in the earth: lo, there thou hast that is thine.
> (Matthew 25:24-25)

This servant displayed an attitude of fear, which will cause either inaction or improper action. The servant said, "I know you are a hard man. I was afraid of you, so I went and hid your money. Here, you can have your money back."

A quick look at this and at the Master's response would lead one to think that the Master had been demanding his money back. In actuality, the Master was responding to the servant in the manner he had been spoken to. The master said, "Thou wicked and slothful servant . . . Thou oughtest therefore to have put my money to the exchangers, and then at my coming I should have received mine own with usury [interest]" (Matthew 25:26, 27).

We can have a clearer understanding of what is taking place by looking at Luke 19:22. This verse says, "And he saith unto him, Out of thine own mouth will I judge thee." The Lord responded in a manner that had been predetermined by the attitude and words of the servant. Proverbs 18:20 says, "A man's belly shall be satisfied with the fruit of his mouth." The Word also teaches that we have to eat the fruit produced by the words we speak.

The Master was dealing with the third servant on the basis of the servant's attitude, as expressed in his words. The Master said, in essence, "Since you said this is my money, I will judge you that way. You are lazy, wicked, slothful, and of no use. If the money were mine, you should have at least put it in the bank to draw interest. Then I would have had my money, with interest."

I want to stress that the Master was not saying the money was his. He had delivered it to the servant. The servant determined how he would be judged—by his attitude, his words, and his actions. I believe that if the man had taken the $1,000, entered into business, and lost it all, the Master would have said, "Well done, thou good and faithful servant." At least the man would have been doing something with what had been given to him.

Don't Waste Your Talents and Abilities

Many of God's people have talents and abilities that are not being used, because they are waiting for God to do something.

God has given you talents and abilities. He expects you to put them to use. If you are not busy for the kingdom of God (and I am not talking about full-time ministry), you are slothful and lazy. God never called people to be pew sitters. There is no such office in the New Testament!

God has placed you in a church or ministry that needs your talent and ability to help supply all that is necessary for that ministry (1 Corinthians 12:18).

We see the same truth in Ephesians 4:16. Speaking of the Church, the Apostle Paul said, "The whole body fitly joined together and compacted by that which every joint supplieth, according to the effectual working in the measure of every part, maketh increase of the body unto the edifying of itself in love."

We need each other to get the job done. So put your talent to work and begin producing for the kingdom of God.

4

Use What You Have

Let us examine the two faithful servants and see not only their attitude but also their productivity. Each man was given according to the ability he had.

In Matthew 25:20-23 we saw how the first two servants took the money that had been given them and entered into commerce. They used the money and let it produce for them.

Both men doubled the original amount they had been given. The man with $5,000 went and traded. He entered into business and used his ability to double his original sum. The man who had received $2,000 did the same. He used his money to the best of his ability and it doubled for him.

Now notice that each man was given according to his several abilities. Not only did these men double their money, they doubled their ability. The man who made $10,000 also gained the ability to use that much. The man who made $4,000 also gained the ability to use that much.

There is a principle of operating in life, no matter what you do: If you use what you have to the best of your ability, you will not only double your productivity, you will double your ability.

This is a continuous progression. The man who received the $2,000 and doubled it had a concept working for him. He then had $4,000 and the ability to use that amount. If he continued to use his money to the best of his ability, he would continue to double both his money and his ability. Think of that! He started with 2, then had 4. Next he would have had 8, then 16, then 32, then 64, then 128, and so on.

TAKING TALENTS AND ABILITIES TO HIGHER LEVELS

Can you see the importance of using your talents to the utmost of your ability? You will not only double your productivity, you will double your ability.

We stated earlier that the parables about the kingdom were written to give us the example of how to operate in the kingdom of God. Your effectiveness will be governed by your use of what the Lord has given to you. The Apostle Paul states: "Yet when we are among the full-grown—spiritually mature Christians who are ripe in understanding—we do impart a (higher) wisdom [that is, the knowledge of the divine plan previously hidden]" (1 Corinthians 2:6 *AMP*). This implies that there is something not readily available without some prior knowledge.

In your Christian walk, certain things become clearer as you grow. It must be line upon line, precept upon precept. You are always building upon what you have already learned.

The kingdom of God, the activity of reigning, operates the same way. As you become proficient in one area, you move to the next higher level of proficiency. Once you realize that Jesus is the healer, you pray for the sick and begin to see results. The more results, the greater the degree of accuracy and boldness on your part. But if you never begin, you will never operate in that kingdom principle.

5

It Worked for Me!

I would like to share some personal experiences that will act as windows for you to see this principle of doubling your ability in operation. We learn by both precept and example.

When I was the assistant pastor of a church in Southern California, my responsibilities included preaching once a week in the main service, preaching when the pastor was out of town, overseeing the Sunday school department, and making sure the ushers knew what to do.

After being on staff for about four months, I was asked by the pastor to take over the Bible school. The school was in trouble financially and numerous students were dropping out.

God had given the pastor a vision to train and equip men and women for the ministry with the accurate Word of God. The only way that church knew to do this was by starting a Bible school.

One of the classes was a survey of the Old Testament. In a twelve-week period, the students had to read and outline the entire Old Testament, besides

ATTITUDE OF A SERVANT

learning the kings and prophets of both the northern and southern kingdoms of Israel and Judah. This was quite a bit for the students to do in addition to their other classes. Many of them had not been in Bible school for years.

While talking with the pastor, I suggested that in view of the vision God had given him he needed a training center rather than a Bible school. He agreed, then asked me to take charge.

I thought, "God, You never called me to run a Bible training center: You called me to teach and preach".

This was an attitude I had to deal with. I had no desire to do it and did not think I had the necessary ability. But the ability had to be in me, or the Spirit of God would never have prompted the pastor to ask me to run this important facet of his ministry.

I had to begin by faith. I could easily have said I was not called to start a Bible training center. Instead, I trusted the Lord and relied on Him for wisdom and guidance.

To transform the school into a training center, it was necessary to develop a curriculum, set a fee structure, design advertising material, and form a schedule of classes. By spending time in prayer, I was given direction from the Lord.

The result was a nine-month, four-hour-per-week course taught on Saturdays. It consisted of three twelve-week semesters with four classes taught each semester. The first year we graduated 27 students. The second year we enrolled 220 students and graduated 200.

The success of the school did two things: It got men and women trained in the Word and out working for the Lord, and it produced $40,000 for the church in a nine-month period.

I soon learned about my productivity and my ability.

The initial curriculum (12 classes) was being used successfully, and I was extremely happy. There would be no need to fool around with curriculums anymore, I thought, but I was wrong. The pastor asked me to produce a curriculum for a nine-month school, with classes meeting five days a week and three hours a day. By relying upon the ability God had placed inside me, I developed the curriculum for this school. I had doubled my ability! I was being more productive for the kingdom of God.

DOUBLING AGAIN AND AGAIN

Shortly afterward, I began to travel and teach God's Word. I thought I would never have to develop another curriculum, but God had other thoughts in mind. In October of 1979 while I was attending the first meeting of the International Convention of Faith Churches and Ministers in Fort Worth, Texas, the Lord told me I would be involved with starting training centers throughout the nation and around the world. At the same time, the Lord dealt with me about moving to Tulsa, Oklahoma.

When I finished the initial five-day-a-week course for the training center in California, I did not realize the impact this would have upon my life and ministry. It was then that I left California and moved to Tulsa.

Once I had settled my family in Tulsa, I met with the pastors of a large fellowship there. One of these men mentioned their Bible school that was to open in Jamaica in September, 1980. They had the facilities, the students, and the teachers. It was ready to start. All they needed was a curriculum.

Together, we produced a nine-month Bible course. It was a curriculum incorporating 162 lessons on faith,

162 lessons on spiritual emphasis subjects (e.g., the blood covenant, gifts of the Spirit, practical ministries), and 324 lessons on expository and additional classes (e.g., New Testament Survey, Sermon Preparation, The Book of Revelation). This curriculum became the World Outreach Bible Institute, now being used extensively around the world. At the request of many pastors in America, the curriculum has been modified for use there.

This personal experience ties in directly with the object of Jesus' parable in Matthew 25—every man was given according to his own ability. God knew the ability I had, so He allowed me to produce according to that ability.

By being faithful to what God had for me to do, I constantly doubled my ability and my effectiveness. If I had trained and sent out ten ministers, I would have increased my effectiveness tenfold. The people I trained would affect others that I could never reach personally by going out and holding seminars. I have, in essence, duplicated myself in those who have been trained with the curriculum.

Numerically, we have seen outstanding results. In California the first graduating class to use the initial curriculum numbered 27 students. The second class graduated 200, all from the Southern California area. The next group using an expanded curriculum included graduates from the schools in England, Guatemala, and Jamaica. We now have students enrolled in schools throughout the world.

Can you see the parallel in this? By remaining faithful and diligent, and doing what is at hand to do to the best of your ability, you will double your ability and effectiveness. Amen Alleluia

09/23/2014

6

Singleness of Heart

The pastor of a church in California was on the road quite a bit, but I was always in the office. A lady kept calling for counseling. Whenever she called, she first tried to get the pastor. Then she would ask for one of the other ministers.

Usually, neither of them was in, so she would say, "Well, who is there?" The receptionist would say, "Mike is here." So, she would talk to me. I gave her good counsel—whatever the Word said about her problem. Then we would pray.

I was doing the will of God from my heart, and doing it with singleness of heart. She would say to me, "I tried to get the pastor, but he's not available! Then I tried to get one of the other ministers, but he wasn't available either. So, because you're here, I'm stuck with you."

But she began to change and grow. And it was a thrill for me to be able to watch her!

One day she decided to sell her house. After the house was sold, she came to church on a Sunday morning with an envelope. As she walked up to me, she was all smiles.

She said, "It's my joy and pleasure to do this, because no one else was ever around when I needed them. But you were always there. Here, I want you to have this."

I opened the envelope, and inside was a check for $5,000! Oh, I tell you—that was enjoyable! But I'd been available for two years whenever she called. So do the will of God from your heart, because God will cause you to be rewarded.

SELFLESS COMMITMENT

One word in the New Testament that deals with being a servant and giving service is *doulos*, which implies a totally selfless commitment to another. Vine says this word is used "frequently indicating subjection without the idea of bondage."[2]

In other words, everything that the servant does is a totally selfless commitment to another, to his master. Everything he does is designed to bring honor and glory to his master and not to himself. He's interested in doing whatever he can to benefit his master, not what will benefit himself.

Although a *doulos* is totally subjected to his master, there's no bondage involved at all. In our culture it's hard to conceive of that. Can you imagine being under the total control and influence of someone else without bondage? When Paul talks about being a servant of Jesus Christ, he uses the word *doulos*, yet there's no implication of bondage.

An equivalent Hebrew word was used in the Old Testament and translated "bond slave."[3] In Exodus 21:16, we read:

Now these are the judgments which thou
shalt set before them.

If thou buy an Hebrew servant, six years he
shall serve: and in the seventh he shall go out
free for nothing.

If he came in by himself, he shall go out by
himself: if he were married, then his wife
shall go out with him.

If his master have given him a wife, and she
have born him sons or daughters; the wife
and her children shall be her master's, and he
shall go out by himself.

And if the servant shall plainly say, I love
my master, my wife, and my children; I will
not go out free:

Then his master shall bring him unto the
judges; he shall also bring him to the door, or
unto the door post; and his master shall bore
his ear through with an aul; and he shall
serve him forever.

In other words, they pierced the ear lobe as a
sign of total servitude. The concept here is that if a love
relationship developed and the servant did not want to
go free, he was taken to the judges in the city where he
made known his desire to become a bondservant to his
master.

A hole was then made in his ear as a legal sign.
That hole would signify the fact that this person had
ceased to exist as himself and now was to be totally
identified with his master.

He didn't just serve the man and work for wages, but became totally identified with, and one with his master. No longer was he just a servant but a member of the household, part of the family. He would never leave, and his master became totally responsible for his every need. (Philippians 4:19 says, "But my God shall supply all your need according to his riches in glory by Christ Jesus.")

A similar passage to the one in Exodus is found in Deuteronomy 15:12-13: "And if thy brother, an Hebrew man, or an Hebrew woman, be sold unto thee, and serve thee six years; then in the seventh year thou shalt let him go free from thee." Now notice this: "And when thou sendest him out free from thee, thou shalt not let him go away empty."

After six years of service, if a servant wanted to go free, the master wasn't to send him away empty-handed. He wasn't to say, "You came here with nothing, and you're leaving with nothing:" Instead, he was to say, "You came here with nothing, and now I'm sending you out increased with goods. I'm giving you a part of everything you've helped me to gain."

Verse 15 of that chapter continues, "And thou shalt remember that thou wast a bondman in the land of Egypt, and the Lord thy God redeemed thee: therefore I command thee this thing to day."

In other words, God told the Israelites that when they set free a servant, it was to be as it was when God set them free from the land of Egypt. He sent them out with silver, gold, jewels, cattle, and sheep. He increased them. So when a servant left, they were to make sure he went out well blessed.

And it shall be, if he say unto thee, I will not go away from thee; because he loveth thee and thine house, because he is well with thee;

Then thou shalt take an aul, and thrust it through his ear unto the door, and he shall be thy servant for ever. And also unto thy maidservant thou shalt do likewise. (Deuteronomy 15:16-17)

Picture this: You're ready to send your servant off well supplied. You're going to increase him in cattle, in grain, in wine, and in goods. He's going away with his pockets full and overflowing. But a love relationship has developed between you. He says, "All that increase is great, but I don't want to go. I want to serve you."

That must mean the master has taken good care of that individual. The master is saying, "Here, you can have all this," The individual is saying, "Hey, listen, it's better off here than it is out there in the world."

If you have a company and you want to keep employees, make it so attractive for them and take such good care of them that, if somebody comes and offers them more money, they won't leave, because money isn't the most important thing to them.

NOT ENOUGH SERVANTS

We've been talking about singleness of heart, about having a servant's attitude, about having the determination that you are going to serve, then serving with singleness of heart. One of the problems within the Body of Christ today is that we don't have many servants. We have a lot of ministers, but not many servants.

Paul says in Philippians 2:19-21, "But I trust in the Lord Jesus to send Timotheus shortly unto you . . . For I have no man likeminded, who will naturally care for your state. For all seek their own, not the things which are Jesus Christ's." Paul said the only person he could send them was Timotheus (Timothy), because he was the only one available who would be concerned about them and not about his pocketbook.

Timothy had singleness of heart, so did Paul. And both considered themselves servants. When you're a servant, God can use you because you'll be faithful. Paul says in 1 Corinthians 4:2 that faithfulness is required of a steward, a servant of God. There's no higher calling in life than to be a servant of God and to be faithful or single-minded. But you cannot be this kind of servant until you're full of the life and nature of God, until you have the mind of Christ.

MADE FREE TO BE A SERVANT OF GOD

Paul talks about another attribute of a servant of God in Romans chapter 1. He says we're to live a "separated life," to be "separated unto the gospel of God." Now some people have a funny idea of what that means. Time and again I've heard people say something like, "I'm free. I don't have to go to church. I've got liberty. Jesus told me to stand fast in the liberty wherewith Christ made me free. I'm not going to be entangled in the yoke of bondage again. Nobody is going to put bondage on me."

When did going to church become bondage? Paul said, "All things are lawful unto me, but all things are not expedient" (1 Corinthians 6:12). Also, when some people say they're "free," apparently they mean they're free to sin, to do things they don't need to be doing.

"I'm free. Therefore I can go down to the bar and drink a couple of glasses of wine or have a drink or two." The Bible also says, "But now being made free from sin, and become servants to God, ye have your fruit unto holiness, and the end everlasting life" (Romans 6:22).

You've been made free, not to sin or to do your own thing, but to become a servant of God. You aren't free to do anything that you might want to do. Before you were recreated, you didn't have a choice. Your nature caused you to sin. You were in bondage to satan. Now you're free not to sin. That's what true freedom is. Being a servant is a thing of freedom.

Jesus had the attitude of a servant. Matthew 10:24-25 "The disciple is not above his master, nor the servant above his lord. It is enough for the disciple that he be as his master, and the servant as his lord."

People get the inflated idea that because they hold a certain office in the Body, or operate in certain ministries of the gifts of the Spirit, that they're something great. Not so. Jesus said, "The disciple is as his master, the servant as his lord."

7

Functions of a Servant

I have been teaching for many years about the ministry gifts, and about the need to honor those gifts. It's true that we do need to honor the ministry gifts, because they're gifts to the church from God. They're given to minister to us and cause us to be effective.

When we receive ministry gifts, we're saying to God, "Thank You for the opportunity You've given me to administer this gift to the church." But you have to receive it, or it's not useful to you and you can not make it useful to the church.

Some individuals have a mistaken attitude about the gifts of the Spirit. Instead of understanding that the gift is to the church, and they're just to administer it, they get the idea that they are the gift!

They act like this: "I'm a gift. You'd better treat me right, because I'm a gift to you." Or like this: "Don't come near me. Don't touch me—I'm a gift. I don't want to talk to the people, I'm going to go pray. I'm going to be God's person of faith and power."

Have you seen that kind of person? Instead of being good stewards and concerned about God's requiring an account of the administration of the gift He gave them for the church, these people are all flash and no bang. They think they're faith and power when they're really just paste and flour.

While ministering in a powerful three-day meeting for a friend of mine in the state of Washington, he kept shaking his head. Finally, I asked him, "Brother, what's wrong?"

He said, "You're not like any other traveling minister that I know."

I said, "What do you mean?"

He explained that all the traveling ministers whom he had come in contact with would wait in the wings until the worship service was over. When it came time to introduce them, then they would appear. They would minister the Word, minister to the people, then quickly go out the back door. They were untouchable.

But I have a pastor's heart and I love the people. I don't want to run out the back door. I want to fellowship with people. Now, understand, some individuals have to leave quickly—and I've had to modify my normal behavior overseas, where you have crowds of 10,000 to 15,000 people in a meeting.

In very large meetings, the evangelist can't stick around to fellowship. If he fellowshipped with one, he would leave out the multitude. The only way to treat everybody fairly is not to give anyone special attention. But in small to medium-sized meetings, sometimes staying away from the people is a sign of a wrong attitude.

Paul said, "What I am is a servant. I'm not anything else. I'm a servant of Jesus Christ." When I realize that I'm a servant, it takes away all the inner turmoil and strife, all the competition. Because I'm a servant, I'm responsible only for carrying out the instructions of my Master.

Secondly, in Romans 1:1 Paul said he was called to be an apostle. "*To be*" is in italics in the Bible, so it's not in the original Greek, but added by the translator for our understanding. The passage could be read this way: "Paul, a servant of Jesus Christ, called an apostle." Paul was saying, "What I am is a servant. How I function is as an apostle."

In Ephesians 4:11, it says that Jesus gave gifts unto men: "And he gave some, apostles; and some, prophets; and some, evangelists; and some, pastors and teachers." We call these the five-fold ministry gifts.

Then in 1 Corinthians 12:28, Paul says, "And God hath set some in the church, first apostles, secondarily prophets, thirdly teachers, after that miracles, then gifts of healings, helps, governments, diversities of tongues."

We used to try to make those two verses mesh in this way:

First Corinthians 12:28 says "apostles, prophets, and teachers," so those three are taken care of. But it also says "miracles, and gifts of healings," so that has to be the evangelist. Exciting things happen for the evangelist. Then we have "helps, governments, and diversities of tongues," so that must be the ministry of the pastor.

In recent years, however, we've learned that there's a ministry of helps, a supernatural ministry where an individual is called by God.[4] There are people who get involved in helping, but who aren't called specifically into such a ministry. But those who are placed by God into this kind of ministry are just as important as the apostle, prophet, evangelist, pastor, or teacher.

FUNCTIONS ARE NOT TITLES

Such as the ministry of government, administration or "ruling," and the ministry of tongues, these verses about ministries left people with many questions. I used to ponder over Ephesians 4:11 and 1 Corinthians 12:28, but they just wouldn't fit together. Something was wrong with my understanding.

I was in a service on a Sunday morning when the pastor made this statement in his preaching, "You know, I've been studying, praying, and asking God about Ephesians 4, and the Lord said to me: 'I never meant those as positions or titles. I meant those as job descriptions. People have taken their job description and elevated it, and said that's what they are. No, those listings are just <u>descriptions</u> of their jobs.'"

Those ministries are functional titles, names designating where an individual functions, not what an individual is.

During this century, the Holy Spirit has emphasized certain ministries. He's emphasized the apostle's ministry and the prophet's ministry. It seemed everyone wanted to be an apostle or prophet. Nobody wanted to be a pastor.

Then there came an emphasis on the pastor's ministry. Now we have a whole generation of people walking around saying, "I'm an apostle, I'm a prophet, I'm a pastor, I'm an evangelist, I'm a teacher, I'm this, I'm that—I'm . . ." The big "I," the big "me." And where's Jesus?

Paul was saying in Romans 1:1 that he was a servant who functioned as an apostle, "a sent one." When I become a love slave of Jesus Christ, when everything I do is viewed in relationship to causing His will to be done, then my function does not matter, because my function is not what I am, it's what I do.

Today I learn with singleness of Heart of motive

When people get upset because they're working as a janitor, it's because they believe a janitor is what they are. That's not what they are, that's just where they are functioning. Your function is not you. You're a servant of Jesus Christ. What does it matter how you function if you're doing it with singleness of motive, doing it as unto the Lord, doing the will of God from singleness of heart?

As a servant of Jesus, your function is determined by Him, the Master, and not by yourself. The servant is viewed in relationship to his Master. You're not viewed by God in relationship to your work, but in relationship to Jesus.

It doesn't matter how you function: apostle, prophet, evangelist, pastor, teacher, janitor, counselor, usher, host, hostess, or anywhere else it helps. It doesn't matter, because what you are is a servant.

When God dealt with me about the idea of the attitude of a servant, I got out my Strong's Concordance and wrote down every Scripture reference that had the word *servant* in it. Then I went through my Bible and put an asterisk by the references on my list that applied, crossing out the ones that didn't.

When I came to Romans 1:1, I read it and started to cross it out. But the Spirit of the Lord said, "No, go back and read it again." I said, "Well, it doesn't say anything." The Lord said, "Go back and read it again."

Romans 1:1 is a salutation. It's the very beginning of the long letter we know as a "book." And I used to read the salutations the same way I read the genealogy of Christ in Matthew and Luke . . . "begat, begat, begat, begat, begat, begat." I read through it quickly.

I had done this with Romans 1:1—"Paul, a servant of Jesus Christ, called to be an apostle, separated unto the gospel of God." I would try to go on, but God just kept bringing me back to it. I decided to meditate on it, because apparently there was something I wasn't seeing.

When my eyes finally were opened to what the verse really was saying, it was 2 A.M. I had to keep quiet because I was ministering in New Jersey and staying in the pastor's home, but it sure was hard to be silent! Here, in one verse of Scripture—a salutation, at that—you see the whole heart and attitude of the Apostle Paul.

In that one verse, he tells us everything we need to know to be successful. He tells us who he is, how he functions, and how he lives. He was a servant functioning as an apostle and living separated from the world.

I came out of the Hippie culture of the 1960s. In that era, we were trying to "tune in, turn on, and drop out." We were experimenting with mind-altering drugs in an attempt to find out who we were. It was a search for identity. But you can't find out who you are until you're born again. Then you find out who you are in Christ. Once you find that out, then you can begin to do something for God.

Even in the Body of Christ, a lot of people are trying to find out who they are: "Who am I? What am I? Who am I, God?" Paul answered that question for all of us in Romans 1:1. What I am and who I am is a servant of God.

Paul said, "I am a *doulos*, a bondservant." In other words, "I am Paul, the *doulos*, the servant of Jesus Christ. I am Christ's servant, God's servant. I am a love servant. When Christ set me free on the road to Damascus, I chose to be His servant for life. Now I don't live, He lives in me. What I am is a servant."

8

Elements of Servanthood

Some people change their attitudes toward me when they find that I am the author of Supportive Ministries. Sometimes they change their attitude when they find I am on the staff of a large ministry. And that isn't the right attitude.

I'm not viewed in relationship to my work. I'm viewed in relationship to my Master. I'm a servant of Jesus Christ. When you realize that you're a servant, and that's who you are, then your function doesn't matter because the function is determined by the Master. You're not viewed in relationship to your function, you're viewed in relationship to your Master.

"Oh, you work for that ministry?"

"Yes."

Then someone thinks, "I'd better treat him well, because he works for that large church."

That's the wrong attitude. You have to treat me well because I'm a servant of Jesus Christ.

I was teaching in a place one time, and they put me in an economy motel. I went over to the church and talked with the associate pastor. I said, "Brother, I'm not trying to cause any problems. But I've been on the road two weeks. I appreciate the room you gave me, but it's quite small. There's another motel right down the road that has larger rooms and better facilities. I'd rather stay there. I'll pay the difference. I'm not concerned about that. I just would like a comfortable place to stay."

He said, "No problem."

They put me up at the other motel and took care of the bill. I was talking with the associate pastor later that week, and he asked me several things about the traveling ministry. Accommodations was one of the things he wanted to know about.

I said, "Just use this rule of thumb: How would you like to be treated? A traveling minister spends his time on the road. He's in one motel room after another after another. Where would you want to stay if you were constantly away from home and living in hotels? Would you like to stay in a small room where everything is cramped, or would you like to have someplace where you could walk and pray and have a little bit of space?"

He said, "Ah, ha! I see."

So I believe it will be better in the future for all the others who go to minister in that church. I could have had the attitude, "Well, how dare you put me in such a small room. This is beneath my dignity."

But I didn't approach it that way at all. I approached it with an attitude of consideration for my hosts, by offering to pay the difference out of my own pocket.

FUNCTIONS CHOSEN BY GOD

We're servants of God and viewed in relationship to that. What we do, and how we function doesn't matter. When we're viewed in relationship to God, He'll cause us to function in whatever capacity He needs at that given point in time.

You might function primarily as a teacher, which is my primary function in the Body. But I'm not a teacher, I'm a servant. If I get my mind set that, "I'm a teacher, I'm a teacher, I'm a teacher," and I believe that's all I am, I've just cut myself off from God using me in any other way but as a teacher.

But when I say, "I'm a servant," then my function becomes determined by the Master and not by me. God can have me function as a servant, or as an apostle, or as a prophet.

At one church in New Jersey, the Lord has used me several times as a prophet. Did I try to be? No. Did they pray that I would be a prophet to them? No. But I've been there several times, and each time the Lord has used me as a prophet to set some things right.

It began with a three-day seminar on the ministry of helps. I didn't know they were having problems. I made a simple statement, and I said it just like this: "If you don't agree with the vision of the pastor, there's the back door. Don't let it hit you on the way out."

But then I explained: "Now, what I mean to say is that if you can't agree with the pastor's vision, you need to find some place where you can agree. You need to find another place to hook up. So there's the door. Don't let it hit you. Don't make problems. Just resign."

That week, eleven of his workers resigned. He called me the next week and said, "Well, brother, your seminar was a turning point."

I said, "Oh, really?" At first I thought, "Great!"

But then he said, "Yes, I had eleven workers leave."

I sighed, "Oh."

He explained, "But the next Sunday morning, God gave us fifty new people." They were excited.

ELEMENTS OF SERVANTHOOD

Another time when I was going to be in that town, the same congregation asked me to come and minister. They purposely would not tell me what was going on. They were believing God was going to use me to take care of all the problems!

I prayed, "Oh, dear God, I don't think I want to preach tonight."

When they asked what I would preach on, I told them I would preach on the mercy of God.

They questioned, "Are you sure?"

Inspite of their question, I preached on mercy, and it handled the problems. I got off on what I thought was a side trail. Glory! A bunch of people rose up after that and were angry. They went to the pastor and said, "How dare you tell him everything that's going on in this church? You told him what was going on, and you told him what to say!"

Because the Holy Spirit hit everyone and exposed everything through my sermon, they thought the pastor had set them up to be preached at. Four families left, but the next week 100 new people came to the church.

So the third time I was there, they said, "Well, praise God! Brother Mike is coming. Bring your asbestos suits. We love to be corrected and rebuked by the Word."

When the leaders told me how they'd promoted my visit, I thought nobody would show up. But the place was full, and the same thing happened again. Problem people left, and God added 50 new people.

To that church, I functioned as a prophet. The Spirit of God would just show me things and nail them.

I didn't go in there trying to be a prophet. I would pray, "God, give me a nice, simple, sweet message. I want to be loved. I don't want to be known as the guy that brings the fire."

I ministered there about three times, and that church increased by 200 people. The increase didn't come by my being there. The increase came after I functioned there as a prophet and the dead weight left.

To that church I was a prophet. Am I a prophet? No. I'm a servant of Jesus Christ. As a servant, I'll function any way the Master needs me to function.

Dick Mills, who functions primarily as a prophet, asked me to share with his staff about the attitude of a servant. When I shared the concepts that are in this book, and we talked afterwards, he said, "You've answered a question for me."

He explained, "I usually stay in the ministry of a prophet, but I've gone into some churches where all I could do was teach. I'd go somewhere else and have apostolic power. I'd go someplace else, and all I could do was preach an evangelistic message. I'd go someplace else, and all I could do was pastor the people. What you shared today enlarged my perspective. I'm a servant, and as a servant, my function doesn't matter. God can use me in whatever function is necessary at the time."

But you can't be like that until you're a servant. All those people who are running around saying they're this, that, and the other thing are sadly mistaken. They're servants.

People need to understand and recognize where they primarily function, but the easiest way of doing it is by realizing their status as servants. When they begin to operate as servants, they begin to serve God in the way which He desires. Their function will not remain the same, it will constantly change.

PERSONAL EXAMPLES

I'd been on the staff of a Full Gospel church for four and a half years, working my way up from janitor to associate pastor. Then I spent four and a half months with a Jewish outreach ministry.

In this latter ministry, they didn't believe certain things that I believed, and it got to the point where the differences were going to cause a split.

I was teaching the truths of the integrity of God's Word, restored by the Holy Spirit to the Body of Christ during the last 50 years, and they were teaching against it. I would say one thing, and the senior pastor would say the opposite.

People would come to me saying, "What's going on? We can see in the Word that what you're saying is true, but he's against it. What are we going to do?"

I started praying about the situation. Then I went to the pastor, resigned, and left town. Six months later, they asked me to come back and preach. I preached, and the Holy Spirit turned that place right-side-up.

As a result, some four months later, the pastor brought in an associate who understood things of the Spirit. But he wasn't ready to receive the truth of the Word while I was there. So rather than cause division or strife, I left.

Soon after, I was asked to be the Assistant Pastor of a growing church in Palos Verdes, CA. I preached all the time, almost every Sunday evening and Wednesday evening. I was thanking God that He called me to preach and teach. That's all I wanted to do.

Then in August of 1977, after I'd been with that church for six months, God began to deal with me about administration. But I didn't want to hear it. In fact, I remember the Wednesday night when He first spoke to me about adding administration to my function.

The Lord said, "I want you to tell the Senior Pastor that I'm going to send him an administrator whose salary is already paid." I remember arguing with the Lord over that. I thought, "That's ridiculous."

But I went to him, and I said, "The Lord just told me to tell you this. It might sound ridiculous, and I don't know how He's going to do it, but He said that He's going to send you an administrator whose salary is already paid."

Little did I know that it was me! A few weeks later, on a Sunday morning, the Senior Pastor asked if my wife, Martha, was in the service. When I told him she was, he said, "I've got to minister to you. I have a word from the Lord for you."

I thought, "Glory to God, it's time for my radio ministry." That was a big thing back then. Everybody was going on the radio. I thought I would have a radio ministry and maybe a newsletter.

So he called Martha and me up in front of the whole congregation, and said, "Mike, are you willing to be an administrator?" And, almost immediately, I responded, "Yes."

I'd made an adjustment in my attitude. It took me about three seconds to make that adjustment on the inside. Then I said, "Yes."

And the Spirit of the Lord ministered through him and said, "If you'll be faithful for two years, I'll release you to that which you desire to do."

At that time, I desired to travel and teach. But I stayed with him, pastored the church, and ran his training center. We gained national prominence. And it was interesting that in August, 1979—two years later to the day—I left that ministry and began to travel.

I traveled across the nation for a year with tremendous results: miracles, signs, and wonders. Then I became a member of the Pastoral Staff of Faith Christian Fellowship in Tulsa and Dean of the School of Helps.

I had not even gotten to preach in the church before I became a staff member. Then they let me preach once in the church when everybody was out of town. Should I cry and complain? No. God told me to go serve the pastor, so I went to serve the pastor.

CALLED TO PASTOR

Then one day the Spirit of the Lord told me, "You're going to be one of the pastors."

When He told me that, I said, "Sure. I'm willing." But I didn't run to the pastor and tell him that I was going to be one of his pastors. No way!

I put the prophetic word to me on the shelf, and said, "OK, God, I know Your voice, and I believe this is You. Now You're going to have to tell the pastor."

One of the biggest thrills I've ever had came while I was sitting at breakfast with the pastor one morning. He said, "Mike, have you ever considered pastoring?"

I knew already where he was going with that question, but I said, "If you mean going out and pastoring my own church, no. That's not what God has in mind for me."

He said, No, I didn't mean that. Mike, I need you to pastor our South Worship Hall. Would you rather do that, or continue doing what you are called and anointed to do: set up Bible schools across the nation and around the world? Which would you rather do? the pastor continued. "I know this is going to be a hard decision for you to make. Go ahead and pray about it."

I answered, "I don't need to pray about it, Pastor."

He looked surprised and replied, "You don't?"

"No. God called me to serve you. What do you need me to do?"

"Pastor the church."

"Then that's what I'll do." I then told him what the Lord had told me about being one of the pastors.

He then started telling me all the reasons why I should stay with the Bible schools—he wanted me to be sure in my own mind and spirit about the change of functions.

I interjected, "Wait a minute, Pastor. I'm smart enough to realize that if God told me to serve you, and I serve you in whatever capacity is necessary, it will work out for the best. Even if I can't devote time to the schools now, they'll be farther down the road when I finish doing what you need than if I were to act in disobedience and work on them that whole time."

That statement is true. I haven't done a lot to our Bible school curriculum, but many things have transpired. We've obtained a relationship with a university in Hawaii that offers long distance learning programs for completing degree work. They have agreed to accept our courses as part of the credit necessary for individuals to obtain a degree in Biblical Studies with them.

WE HAVE ALSO GONE INTERNATIONAL!

The curriculum has also been translated into Italian, Norwegian, Spanish, French, Russian, Polish, and Portuguese. The material is being used in the Philippines, Norway, Portugal, Kenya, England, Mexico, Ecuador, Lithuania, Poland, USA, Guatemala, Honduras, and Belize.

Now you see, God called me to start training centers. But I'm a servant. And by serving my pastor and doing what he needs to have done, more doors opened up for the Bible school curriculum than you can imagine. And I haven't had to pursue one of them! They came to me.

The truth of this principle has allowed the schools to expand at a rapid rate. The Lord directed my family and me to move to New Jersey. We obeyed the Lord, and He began to open doors I had previously dreamed of, but did not see how they could ever become reality.

The pastor of a church, Faith Fellowship Ministries, welcomed us with open arms. He encouraged me concerning the Bible schools and made all his television equipment available. This opened a whole new vista, and increased the accessibility of the curriculum. We now have our material available on video, which enables churches to open a Bible school while they are developing a teaching staff. The curriculum available on video also provides the avenue to have a video as well as'an audio correspondence school.

It has taken many years to reach the point where I am now. I consider all those years as preparation for what I'm currently doing. If I had not been faithful to do what was at hand to do, I would still be back at square one.

PAUL'S DEVELOPMENT INTO HIS MINISTRY

In Acts 9, Paul was called as an apostle. In Acts 13, he was separated. That wasn't long, just 15 years. First he was called, then 15 years later was separated to the office or ministry that he had been called into.

In fact, after he was called of God, the first thing he did was witness. Later he served as a teacher. Then he functioned as a prophet. After that, God thrust him back into what he'd been called to do 15 years before.

But, because he was a servant, Paul said, "And I thank Christ Jesus our Lord, who hath enabled me, for that He counted me faithful, putting me into the ministry" (1 Timothy 1:12). So, you see, when you count yourself as a servant, when you understand that a servant is who you are, then God can use you.

9

Faithfulness Makes the
Difference

I asked the Lord one time why He had brought me to serve in various ministries, and why I was able to have such impact in the area of training people with the Word. His answer shocked me at first.

I wanted Him to say it was because of my great teaching ability, or because I was extremely anointed, or because I had so much knowledge. Instead, He said, "I brought you here because I know you will be faithful. You will not only start the job, but you will see the job to completion." He said that because I was faithful, I was chosen.

In Matthew 20:16 and 22:14, the Scriptures state, "Many are called, but few are chosen." I used to ponder over this portion of Scripture. I knew that God was not respectful of people. He would not choose one over another. Therefore, I thought, it had to be something on our part that made the difference between being called and being chosen. The one element that makes the difference is the element of faithfulness.

In 1 Corinthians 4:2 Paul states: "Moreover it is required in stewards, that a man be found faithful." He says that God requires a steward, a minister of His, to be faithful. He did not say you had to be intelligent, be eloquent of speech, or have great natural ability. He said you had to be <u>faithful</u>. As I studied the Scriptures, I found one outstanding element in the lives of God's men: faithfulness.

Over the last 30 years, I have seen many individuals with the call of God upon their lives who are doing nothing for the Lord. When I compared those lives with the ones of those who are working for God, I discovered that the difference was faithfulness (or the lack of it.) Many who were called upon by God were not chosen for His work because they refused to be faithful. Because of this, they were not promoted into what the Lord had designed for them. Most are sitting around today, waiting to be thrust out into their worldwide teaching and miracle ministry, refusing to do anything less than having top billing and being the one everyone looks to for the answers.

The Scriptures say that many are called, but few are chosen. Faithfulness makes the difference.

The word *called* means 'to be invited or summoned.' The word *chosen* means 'to be selected.' you can see from the definitions, as there is a difference between being called and being chosen. You determine the outcome by your faithfulness.

Webster's Dictionary defines *faithful* as 'firmly adhering to duty; constant in performance of duties; consistent, reliable, dependable.' A synonym for faithful is loyal. The word *loyal* is defined as 'faithful adherence to a person; faithful to constituted authority; faithful; having an obligation to defend or support.'

These two words—*faithful* and *loyal*—may seem insignificant, but they play a major part in the success or failure of your life and ministry. Faithfulness is a character trait, a fruit of the recreated human spirit, that is evidenced throughout the Word of God in reference to men who were successful.

This can be seen readily in the relationship between Paul and Timothy. Timothy was loyal to Paul. In 1 Corinthians 4:17, Paul describes Timothy as his beloved son, and faithful in the Lord. In Philippians 2:20-23 Paul, speaking about Timothy, states, "For I have no man likeminded, who will naturally care for your state. For all seek their own . . . But ye know the proof of him, that, as a son with the father, he hath served with me in the gospel."

This is an example of loyalty and faithfulness. As a result, Timothy was the only person Paul felt confident to send on important business. He represented Paul and the Lord well.

In dealing with the difference of being called or chosen, it is interesting to look at the life of the apostle Paul. Though he was called to be an apostle in Acts 9, it was not until Acts 13 that Paul was separated for the ministry he had already been called to: "Separate me Barnabas and Saul (Paul) for the work whereunto I have called them" (Acts 13:2). It was after this that Barnabas and Paul began their first missionary journey to the provinces of Galatia, a journey that took two years.

When you realize that the time between Acts 9 and Acts 13 is 15 years, you can see that Paul did not start out as an apostle. (To compute the time, you use Galatians 1:18 [3 years] and Galatians 2:1 [14 years]—a total of 17 years. Subtract the 2 years Paul spent in his first missionary journey. That leaves 15 years between Paul's being called and his being chosen.)

A common misconception is that when called a person immediately begins to fulfill his ministry. In Paul's life he was faithful as a witness, then as a teacher, then as a prophet for 15 years before he was chosen (separated) for the ministry God had called him to. This time period was a proving time, a time when he was able to make full proof of his ministry.

IMPORTANCE OF FAITHFULNESS

I want to show you another example from the Word that teaches the importance of faithfulness, and the difference between being called and being chosen. This example is seen in the lives and ministries of Elijah and Elisha.

In 1 Kings, chapter 19, Elijah has just come from the slaughter of the prophets of Baal. He has demonstrated that the Lord is the only true God, and Jezebel, King Ahab's wife, wants to kill him for killing all her prophets. Elijah has fled from before her for 40 days.

At Mount Horeb he complains to God that there is no one else that has not bowed to Baal. But God tells him that there are still 7,000 who have not bowed. It is in this setting that the Lord tells Elijah what he is to do. He tells Elijah who to anoint as his replacement: "and Elisha . . . shalt thou anoint to be prophet in thy room" (1 Kings 19:16). The expression *in thy room* means *in your place.*

Elijah obeys the Lord and finds Elisha plowing the field with 12 yoke of oxen. Elijah walks by him and casts his mantle upon him. Elisha, immediately knowing what this means, asks the prophet to let him go back and kiss his mother and father.

Elijah's response is designed to get Elisha to settle in his own mind the question of his calling. Elijah says, "Go back again: for what have I done to thee?" (verse 20).

Elisha went and slew a yoke of oxen. He burned his bridges behind him, then, "he arose, and went after Elijah, and ministered unto him" (verse 21). The word ministered in Hebrew means to do menial service or wait on as a servant. Elisha, the next major prophet of Israel, waited on the prophet Elijah. He was his constant companion. He cooked, cleaned, and carried the material Elijah would take with them on a journey. In short, he did all the menial tasks that were at hand to do.

In 2 Kings 2 we find that the prophet Elijah is going to be taken to heaven and the mantle is going to fall upon his replacement. The time factor between 1 Kings 19 and 2 Kings 2 is 20 years. Elisha had served this man of God for 20 years. Basically for these 20 years, he had been Elijah's servant.

Second Kings 2:1-15 describes Elisha's succession of Elijah as the prophet in the land. It is important that we see the attitudes of Elisha and those around him, then see where God places the premium.

This portion of Scripture mentions "the sons of the prophets," referring to schools set up in Israel to teach young men how to respond to the spirit of God. These schools were located at Bethel and Jericho. When Elijah was going to be taken to heaven, he determined to go to these schools of the prophets. He said to Elisha, "Tarry here, I pray thee" (verse 2). But Elisha's response was, "As the Lord liveth, and as thy soul liveth, I will not leave thee."

When they arrived at Bethel, the sons of the prophets came to Elisha and began to speak to him. I believe their tone was one of contempt and derision. They were probably 'ministering to each other' about who would be the next prophet. They knew Elijah would be taken to heaven and they looked down on Elisha as just a servant.

It was in this tone that they spoke to Elisha: "Knowest thou that the Lord will take thy master from thy head today?" (verse 3). In other words, they were saying, "Are you so spiritually ignorant and dumb? Haven't you learned anything these past 20 years? Don't you realize that your master will be taken to heaven today?"

Elisha responded, "Yea I know it; hold ye your peace" (verse 3). In other words, "Yes, I know it. Why don't you shut up?"

I want us to stop for a moment and consider one other aspect. Though Elisha had served Elijah as a faithful servant for 20 years, there is no record of any miracle Elisha performed or any prophecy he brought forth. There is nothing to indicate that he was to be the next prophet in Israel. This clearly reveals Elisha's faithfulness and loyalty. (How many individuals do you know who would wait 20 years for their ministry to come to the forefront?)

A DOUBLE PORTION

In 2 Kings 2 we see the rewards and results of faithfulness and loyalty. Elisha would not leave Elijah. His attitude was, "God called me to serve you and be the prophet in your room. Until you go to be with the Lord, that is what I am going to do."

Together, they crossed over the Jordan on dry ground. They continued to talk, and finally Elijah said, "Ask what I shall do for thee, before I be taken away from thee. And Elisha said, I pray thee, let a double portion of thy spirit be upon me" (verse 9).

Now let me ask you a question. What would have happened if Elisha had not received a double portion of the prophet's spirit? He was called to be Elijah's replacement. He would be the next prophet in the land. If he had not received the double portion, he would still have walked in the same anointing and the same power as Elijah.

Elisha was asking for the right of the first-born male in the household of Israel: a double portion of the inheritance (Deuteronomy 21:17). In essence, he was saying to Elijah, "You have no wife or children, and I have left all. I am like a son unto you. What I want is the right of the first-born son, the double portion."

Elijah's response was, "Thou hast asked a hard thing: nevertheless, if thou see me when I am taken from thee, it shall be so unto thee; but if not, it shall not be so" (verse 10). He was saying, "We will let the Lord make the decision. If you see me being taken up into heaven, it will be as you desired."

And it came to pass as they went on and talked, that-behold! There appeared a chariot of fire, and horses of fire, and parted them both asunder; and Elijah went up by a whirlwind into heaven.

Elisha saw it, and cried, My father, my father, the chariot of Israel, and the horsemen thereof. (2 Kings 2:11-12)

We must remember that no one in the Old Testament ever called God their Father. They were servants of the Lord, not sons and daughters. This is vital in seeing the answer to Elisha's request.

Elijah and Elisha had developed a father/son relationship which gave Elisha the right to ask for a double portion of the anointing. He had faithfully served the man of God. Even when he knew he was the next prophet, he did not try to exalt himself or attempt to push his ministry. He served the prophet until it was time for him to be exalted, then God exalted him.

When Elisha went back to the Jordan River alone, there were 50 of the sons of the prophets standing far away. They wanted to see something, but they were afar off. Elisha wrapped the mantle, smote the water, and walked across on dry ground (verse 14). The sons of the prophets then all said, "We knew you were the one!"

The double portion Elisha received was in direct relation to his faithfulness. He had a right to the same anointing Elijah had, as he was the one who replaced him, but the relationship that developed between the two because of Elisha's faithful service enabled him to ask for and receive a double portion of the anointing.

In the ministry of Elijah, seven miracles are recorded. In the ministry of Elisha, 14 miracles are recorded. Double the amount! Elisha had doubled his ability and effectiveness by his faithful service to the man of God.

REWARDS OF FAITHFULNESS

I had been invited to hold a teaching seminar in Fresno, California. It was less than one month before we were to move to Oklahoma. I had committed to the meeting, but really did not want to go. Since we were preparing to move to Tulsa, I reasoned that I needed to stay and help my wife get ready for the move.

Every time I prayed about the meeting, the Lord told me to go. I did not want to, but because I had given my word, I went. The main reason I did not want to go was because we had $1,000 in bills and we needed a new car to help us make the move. I had to become willing and obedient.

When the pastor met me at the airport, the first thing he did was rent a car for me. He then registered me at the Hilton Hotel. As I was getting ready to go to my room, the pastor asked if I needed anything. Though I did not have a dollar in my pocket, I told him I did not need anything. He reached into his pocket and pulled out a wad of bills, gave them to me, and said, "Just in case you see anything you might want."

I had never been treated like that before. In most of the places I had ministered they either put me in the homes of the people in the congregation or in run-down motels. I was praising God!

At the first meeting there were about 50 people present. When the pastor received the offering that night, he said, "The offerings during this seminar are going to Brother Mike's ministry." He then proceeded to receive the evening offering.

While he was doing this, the Spirit of the Lord spoke to me and said, "There is a person here who desperately needs a hundred dollars. Take the first hundred dollars from the offering and give it to him." I looked at the size of the crowd and thought, "The first hundred?" It did not look like that much would even come in!

After the offering was received, I asked the pastor, "Did you mean what you said about the offering being mine?" He said, "Yes." So I said to the congregation, "The Lord just spoke to me that someone here is in desperate need of $100. Who is it?" A man on the front row did not even hesitate; his hand was up almost before I completed my sentence. I turned to the pastor and said, "Take the first $100 from the offering and give it to him." Then I went back to my seat.

When I sat down, the Lord said to me, "Son, there is one thing I require in a steward—that he be found faithful. You have been found faithful, and I am going to load it on you."

To think that the Lord had found me faithful, and as a result was going to load it on me. What a humbling experience! I began to weep.

The results of that meeting were tremendous. People were healed, and the power of the Lord was so strong that some people were unable to stand. There was one little boy, about eight or nine years old, who had a club foot. His leg was short. He did not know anything about the power of God. His mother had brought him. The Lord completely healed him. His club foot became normal, and his leg grew.

Financially, the meeting was a success. The offerings totaled over $800. While I was there, $300 came in the mail at home. That was $1,100. All our bills were paid! As I was getting ready to leave, a young man came up and handed me a check for $1,000. He said that the night before, when he and his wife were going to bed, the Lord spoke to them to give that amount to me personally.

The Lord said He was going to load it on me, and He did! I came home with enough to make the down payment on a new station wagon and pay for my family's trip to Tulsa. Since that time, God has continued to be true to His promise, and He keeps loading it on.

It is important that you recognize the place faithfulness holds in the things of God. Faithfulness will keep you on the right track. I have never tried to be in the right place at the right time. I have just been faithful to do what was at hand to do, and the Lord has always placed me in the right place at the right time. If you will be faithful, He will do the same for you!

10

The Paradox of Greatness

The Christian life is full of what seems to be paradoxes or contradictions if judged by the standard of the world's system.

The world says, "Take, or you won't get." The Word says, "Give, and it shall be given unto you" (Luke 6:38). It doesn't say, "Hold back for yourself."

Jesus said that unless you die, you cannot find life. In Romans 8:14-17, God says that we're no longer servants, but children of God. But He tells us that now, because we're fully adopted children, we're to be servants.

Jesus explains the paradox of greatness in Mark 9:30-34:

> And they departed thence, and passed
> through Galilee; and he would not that any
> man should know it.
>
> For he taught his disciples, and said unto
> them, The Son of man is delivered into the
> hands of men, and they shall kill him; and
> after that he is killed, he shall rise the third day.

ATTITUDE OF A SERVANT

> But they understood not that saying, and
> were afraid to ask him.
>
> And he came to Capernaum: and being in the
> house he asked them, What was it that ye
> disputed among yourselves by the way?
>
> But they held their peace: for by the way
> they had disputed among themselves, who
> should be the greatest.

Doesn't that sound like most Christians? "They disputed among themselves who should be the greatest."

And He sat down, and called the twelve, and saith unto them, If any man desire to be first, the same shall be last of all, and servant of all. (Mark 9:35)

If you desire to be great, you must be the servant of all. Jesus' idea of greatness is service. Our idea of greatness is notoriety. The two ideas can go together, because if you're the servant of all, God will promote you to be known by all.

But you'll be known because of your service, not because of yourself. Most of the leaders in the Church today are men who are known because of their service to the Body of Christ.

SERVE FAITHFULLY

One man has taught the same message for more than 40 years. At first, the message he was called to teach wasn't popular. But now it's extremely popular. Neither condition changed him. He's preaching the same thing. He's served God faithfully.

Many in the Body have found that his message works, but it worked just as well for those few who believed it in the early years. Popularity did not make the message any truer, nor him any more faithful.

God's Word works in any age or circumstance, no matter who preaches it, because it's truth. Jesus said, "If you desire to be first, then be the servant of all." And that's true.

When I got to the point where all I cared about was serving Jesus, doing what would please Him and benefit His kingdom, then notoriety began to come. Big deal. Now I couldn't care less.

DISCIPLES CONTINUE TO SEEK GREATNESS

In the tenth chapter of Mark, the discussion was taken up again.

> And James and John, the sons of Zebedee, come unto him, saying, Master, we would that thou shouldest do for us whatsoever we shall desire.
>
> And he said unto them, What would ye that I should do for you?

They said unto him,

> Grant unto us that we may sit, one on thy right hand, and the other on thy left hand, in thy glory. (Mark 10:35-37)

They said, in essence,

> "We don't want much, we just want to sit on Your right and on Your left in glory. We want the two positions of honor and esteem, for eternity. Not much, you know!"

But Jesus said unto them,

Ye know not what ye ask: can ye drink of the cup that I drink of and be baptized with the baptism that I am baptized with?

And they said unto him,

We can. And Jesus said unto them, Ye shall indeed drink of the cup that I drink of; and with the baptism that I am baptized withal shall ye be baptized.

But to sit on my right hand and on my left hand is not mine to give; but it shall be given to them for whom it is prepared.

And when the ten heard it, they began to be much displeased with James and John. (Mark 10:38-41)

Now isn't that just like the multitude? You know why the other disciples got mad at James and John? They were thinking, "How dare they ask for the position of authority, for the position of exaltation?" They thought James and John were going to get a place of honor and they weren't. They probably were mad because they didn't think to ask Jesus for it first.

Remember when Jesus was transfigured? Peter, James, and John were on the mountaintop with Him and saw Him transfigured. When they came down from the Mount of Transfiguration, the disciples were trying to cast the devil out of a man's son, and they couldn't do it.

STRIFE IN THE CAMP

Most of our translations say, "Howbeit this kind goeth not out but by prayer and fasting" (Matthew 17:21).

(Also see Mark 9:29.) Apparently that verse isn't in the original, but was added later. The reason they couldn't cast out the demon is more likely because they were in strife.

They may have been saying, "Peter, James, and John, again. All the time, Peter, James, and John. When Jairus' daughter was raised from the dead, Peter, James, and John got to be in there, and we didn't.

"Man, did you see them on the mountain with thunder and lightning? God appeared just as He did with Moses. All that glory, and Peter, James, and John got to be there. And we've been stuck down here trying to get a dumb devil out of this kid!"

But Jesus called them to him, and saith unto them, Ye know that they which are accounted to rule over the Gentiles exercise lordship over them; and their great ones exercise authority upon them. (Mark 10:42)

He was saying, in essence, "Listen, this is how the world does it. They rule and reign. They exercise that authority with ego, with pride, and if they have a position, they let everybody know about it."

But so shall it not be among you: but whosoever will be great among you, shall be your minister:

And whosoever of you will be the chiefest, shall be servant of all.

For even the Son of man came not to be ministered unto, but to minister, and to give his life a ransom for many. (Mark 10:43-45)

A SERVANT'S ATTITUDE

That last verse summarizes everything that Jesus did, and shows His attitude—the attitude of a servant. He was essentially telling them: "I did not come to be ministered to. If I had wanted to be ministered to, I would have stayed in glory. I had all the angels ministering to me. I didn't come to be ministered to, I came to minister. I didn't come to get. I came to give."

There are a lot of people in the ministry who are trying to be ministered to, and trying to get. People have found out that if they give, it's given to them. They give so they can get. But that's the wrong attitude.

The same idea is brought out in Matthew 23:11, "But he that is greatest among you shall be your servant."

Here Jesus was saying, "You want to be great? You want to be the greatest one? I'll show you how to be the greatest. Be the servant of everyone. The greatest among you shall be your servant."

And whosoever shall exalt himself shall be abased; and he that shall humble himself shall be exalted. (Matthew 23:12)

As amazing as it sounds, I've been in places where ministers argued as to which gift was greatest, and who had authority in that place according to the gift being manifested. They were ready to hurl lightning bolts at each other. "The prophet is greatest!" "No, the apostle is!"

WHO HAS THE HIGHEST AUTHORITY?

In the local church, nobody has greater authority than the pastor. The only churches Paul ever exercised authority over were those he started and, then only until God raised up a pastor for that congregation.

There's a ministry that helped start several churches in Southern California. Their superintendent of churches, who was their "prophet," began going around to the local groups saying, "You're credentialed with us, and I'm here to preach in your church."

Most of the pastors were foolish enough to let him preach. But one pastor stood up to him and said, "Well, that's news to me. I have a message from God to deliver today."

The superintendent said, "But you don't understand. You're ordained with us. I'm a prophet, and I'm here to preach in your church."

Standing firm, the pastor said, "I don't care. I'm the pastor, and you're not preaching in my church this morning. If you want to preach, give me a call, and we'll discuss a date. We'll be more than happy to have you speak sometime, but you're not preaching in my church this morning."

The superintendent persisted, "You don't understand. You're credentialed with us, and I'm a prophet. I'm here to preach."

To which the pastor replied, "Oh, now I understand. I'll take care of it. Just a second." He pulled out his wallet, took out his ministerial card issued by that church, and ripped it into shreds. "There you are," he fumed. "Now, get out of my church." He later was ordained through another organization.

GOD'S SPIRIT GIVES DIRECTION

There's no higher authority than the pastor within the local church. The apostle will go from a church, and God will set prophets within a church. But a prophet doesn't give direction. The Spirit of God gives direction.

The Bible doesn't say, "Those that are led by the prophets are the sons of God." It says that if you're led by the Spirit, you're a son of God. (Romans 8:14)

When we get to heaven and the rewards are passed out, one fellow may say, "Well, Jesus, I'm an apostle." And Jesus will give that person a little reward.

Another guy may say, "I'm a prophet." Jesus will give that guy a little reward.

Then will come a third person who'll say, "Jesus, I'm a servant."

When He hears that, Jesus will turn and say, "Sound the trumpet! Everybody line the streets. We're going to have a parade. We've got a servant!"

Second Peter 1:11 says there will be an abundant entrance opened to you in the kingdom of heaven. Do you know what that means? The gates will be flung wide, and there will be a ticker-tape parade. That's how I want to go in. Jesus said the greatest is going to be the servant of all.

AN EXAMPLE OF A SERVANT'S ATTITUDE

Jesus gave us an example of a servant's attitude, as recorded in John 13:2-4:

> And supper being ended, the devil having now put into the heart of Judas Iscariot, Simon's son, to betray him;

> Jesus knowing that the Father had given all things into his hands, and that he was come from God, and went to God;

> He riseth from supper, and laid aside his garments; and took a towel, and girded himself.

Now history will tell you that the towel He picked up was called the 'servant's towel.' It represented the office of the lowest slave. You couldn't get any lower. The slave that washed and wiped people's feet was the lowest of the low.

That wasn't the bottom of the barrel—it was

underneath the barrel. Jesus, King of kings and Lord of lords, took that servant's towel and began to wash the disciples' feet. He was the King of glory, yet He came to earth and made Himself the lowest of the low.

"After that he poureth water into a basin, and began to wash the disciples' feet, and to wipe them with the towel wherewith he was girded." (John 13:5)

I can just see Peter watching and thinking, "He shouldn't be doing that. He is the Messiah. He can't be doing that."

> Then cometh he to Simon Peter: and Peter saith unto him, Lord, dost thou wash my feet?
>
> Jesus answered and said unto him, What I do thou knowest not now; but thou shalt know hereafter.
>
> Peter saith unto him, Thou shalt never wash my feet. Jesus answered him, If I wash thee not, thou hast no part with me.
>
> Simon Peter with unto him, Lord, not my feet only, but also my hands and my head. (John 13:6-9)

I like Peter's honesty along with his impetuousness. First he tells Jesus, "You'll never wash my feet." He's saying, "You're too good to do that, Lord." But once Jesus tells Peter he will not have any part in the kingdom unless he allows Him to wash his feet, Peter's attitude changes drastically.

He then not only wants his feet washed, but his head and hands as well! In other words, Peter is saying,

"I don't want just a part. I want all." That's a true servant's heart. He wants to serve his master completely. I also like Jesus' response to Peter:

> Jesus with to him, He that is washed needeth not save to wash his feet, but is clean every whit: and ye are clean, but not all.

> For he knew who should betray him; therefore said he, Ye are not all clean. (John 13:10-1)

Jesus used even His last supper with the disciples as an opportunity to teach. He said, in essence, "Listen, you're clean through the Word that I've given to you. When you're born again and filled with the Spirit, you're clean. You're not of this world, but you're in this world. When you get your feet a little bit dirty from walking in the world, the Word I have given you washes them off."

> If we confess our sins, he is faithful and just to forgive us our sins, and to cleanse us from all unrighteousness. (1 John 1:9)

So after he had washed their feet, and had taken his garments, and was set down again, he said unto them,

> Know ye what I have done to you? (John 13:12).

I am sure they were saying, "Yeah, yeah, You washed our feet."

But He said:

> Ye call me Master and Lord: and ye say well; for so I am.

> If I then, your Lord and Master, have washed
> your feet; ye also ought to wash one
> another's feet.
>
> For I have given you an example, that ye
> should do as I have done to you. (John
> 13:13-15)

People have taken that and instituted foot washing services as a doctrine. But He was not talking about having a foot-washing service. What He was saying in essence was, "Listen, I've given you an example. If I, being your Master and Lord, can serve you, then you can surely serve one another."

> Verily, verily, I say unto you, The servant is
> not greater than his lord; neither he that is
> sent greater than he that sent him.
>
> If ye know these things, happy are ye if ye
> do them. (John 13:16-17)

He said, "It is not enough to just know these things, you have got to do them." To be happy, you have to do the works.

UNHAPPY PEOPLE

There are a lot of unhappy people in the body of Christ. Do you want to know why they're unhappy? They're not servants. Some of the most unhappy people I've met are people running around saying, "I'm an apostle! I'm a prophet!" They're miserable and unhappy because they aren't servants.

There are a lot of pastors who aren't servants. They're servants of the people, but not in the way God wants them to be. They're run by people.

The people are miserable, and the pastors are miserable, and all of them think that's the way it's supposed to be. Everyone is miserable, but they think it will be worth it all when they get to heaven. Thank God, it can be worth it all down here!

Jesus tried to give the attitude of a servant to the disciples through His example and teachings. He wanted them to develop an attitude of service that would make them like Him. He said, "Listen, if I, your Master and Lord, have washed your feet, so you ought to do it for one another. I've given you an example. If I can humble Myself and do this, then you can humble yourselves to serve one another. If you want to be great, then be the servant of all."

In other words, your motive in doing things for the Lord is to serve, not to be exalted. When Jesus fed the multitude, He did it to serve them, to meet their needs, not to be exalted. And we should all go and do likewise.

Humility & purity of heart.
Amen Alleluia

Conclusion

The attitude that motivates your behavior will determine the outcome of your situation and, ultimately, of your life. Your attitude controls how others react to you. Your attitude controls how you react to others and to the Lord.

When you have the mind of Christ and consider yourself a servant to Him as Master, you'll be totally identified with Him. Your desire will be to serve, and your life will be one of meeting the needs of others and lifting up Jesus.

The world exalts itself. Satan seeks to exalt himself. The Christian should be exalting Jesus and focusing all attention toward Him.

When you do this, and maintain the proper attitude, the particular functions in which God has sent you becomes your 'jobs' in the Kingdom. Your function is your responsibility, for which you'll have to give an account. It won't become a means for self-exaltation.

It's my prayer that we all develop the attitude of Jesus—the *Attitude of a Servant.*

Biography of Michael Landsman

EDUCATION
BA: in Bible studies, Southern California College (sum cum laude)

MBA: Emphasis in Religious Education, Golden State University

Ph.D: Emphasis Human Development, Golden State University

Ed.D: Education, Honolulu University

MINISTRY EXPERIENCE
Full-time Ministry since April 1972

Harbor Christian Center (1972–1977) (Assemblies of God); Assistant to the Pastor, Youth Pastor, Assistant Pastor

Chaplain: Los Angeles Police Department (1975–1980)

Palos Verdes Faith Center (1977–1979) (Ed Dufresne, Senior Pastor): Associate Pastor, Dean of Bible School, Principal of Christian School

Faith Christian Fellowship (1980–1986) (Buddy Harrison, Senior Pastor): Associate Pastor, International Director of Education, Missions Director, Administrative Pastor, Founder World Outreach Bible Schools, Co-founder of School of Helps

Faith Fellowship Ministries (1986–1996) (Dave Demola, Senior Pastor): Associate Pastor, International Missions Representative, Staff Pastor

Abundant Life World Outreach (1996–2002): Founder/ Director Missions Outreach Organization, Traveling Ministry, International Seminar Speaker, Leadership Training, Ministry of Helps Seminars

Way of Life Community Church (2000–2001): Pastor/ Founder

International Federation of Christian Churches (1997–2002): Member, Conference Speaker

Covenant Ministries International (1994–2002): Founding Trustee, Liaison, International Representative

Staff Minister: RHEMA Bible Church, South Africa (Present)

CREDENTIALS
Christian Worker 1972–1973

Licensed Minister 1974

Ordained Minister: 1975–present

Additional Information

Fellow of International Academy of Education

Academic Field Advisor, Honolulu University

Who's Who in Religion in America (1993 & 1993)

Licensed Pastor Counselor (National Christian Counselors Association)

Completed Jew

AUTHOR

Supportive Ministries – translated into five languages

Attitude of a Servant – translated into three languages

Lord, Increase Our Faith – translated into one foreign language

Doubling Your Ability Through God – translated into one foreign language

Mercy, the Gift Before and Beyond Faith – co-authored with Buddy Harrison – translated into one foreign language

World Outreach Bible School Curriculum – translated into seven languages

PERSONAL INFORMATION

Married Martha Larsen in 1972 – Martha is an anointed Psalmist and Worship leader as well as teacher and conference speaker.

We have three children: Michael Jr. (1976), Linda (1979), Larry (1982), and one grandchild: Amanda (1999).

Michael Jr. is a graduate of RHEMA South Africa

Larry attends RHEMA in South Africa

Linda is a graduate of RHEMA in Tulsa, OK, and is on the worship team of Way of Life in Orlando, FL.

Endnotes

1 Gundry, Robert H., A Survey of the New Testament (Grand Rapids, MI: Zondervan Publishing House, 1982), pg. 144.

2 W. E. Vine, An Expository Dictionary of New Testament Words, (Old Tappan, Fleming H. Revell, 1940), Vol. III, pg. 347.

3 James Strong, Strong's Exhaustive Concordance, Compact Edition, (Nashville, Abingdon, 1890), pg. 84, Hebrew and Chaldee Dictionary.

4 Michael Landsman, Supportive Ministries, (Bridge-Logos Publishers, Newberry, FL, Copyright 1987).